PIANO • VOCAL • GUITAR

THE BEST COUNTRY ROCK SONGS EVER

BEST EVER
Country
ROCK

ISBN 978-1-4803-4068-8

HAL•LEONARD®
CORPORATION

7777 W. BLUEMOUND RD. P.O. BOX 13819 MILWAUKEE, WI 53213

Visit Hal Leonard Online at
www.halleonard.com

ACHY BREAKY HEART
(Don't Tell My Heart)

Words and Music by
DON VON TRESS

might blow _ up and kill this man. Ooh. _____

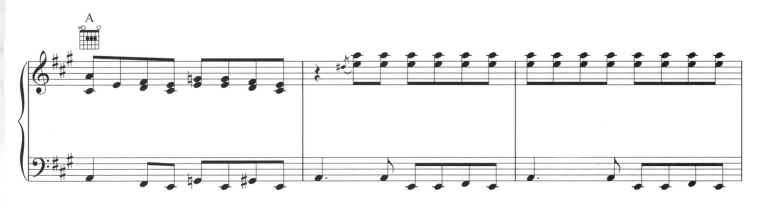

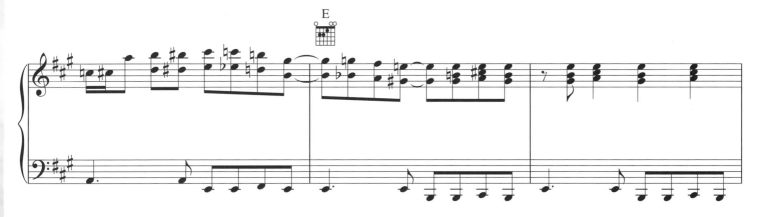

AMIE

Words and Music by
CRAIG FULLER

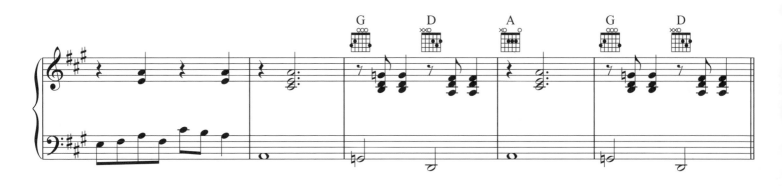

CHAMPAGNE JAM

Words and Music by BUDDY BUIE,
J. COBB and ROBERT NIX

Bright Rock Shuffle

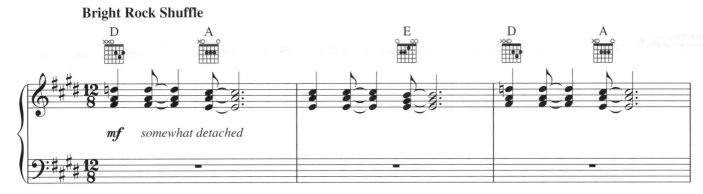

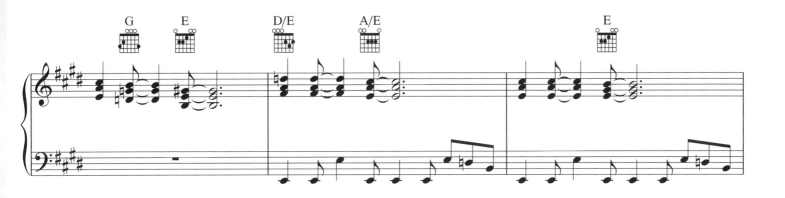

Come on, Ma - ma, give me a break.

Me and the boys are gon - na stay out late.

E7

I can't help it; it's in my bones.
Break out the gui - tars and let's play some blues.

We'll be jam - ming all night long. Gon - na play
Don't want no whis - key; give me some high - class booze. Pour us some

Yeah, __ yeah, _____ yeah, yeah. _____

BOOT SCOOTIN' BOOGIE

Words and Music by
RONNIE DUNN

BREATHE

Words and Music by HOLLY LAMAR
and STEPHANIE BENTLEY

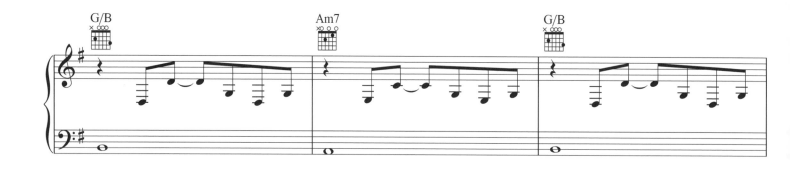

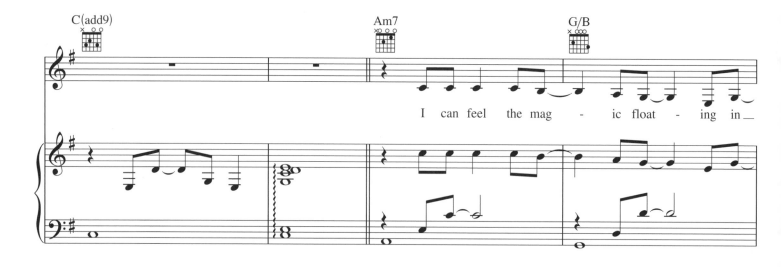

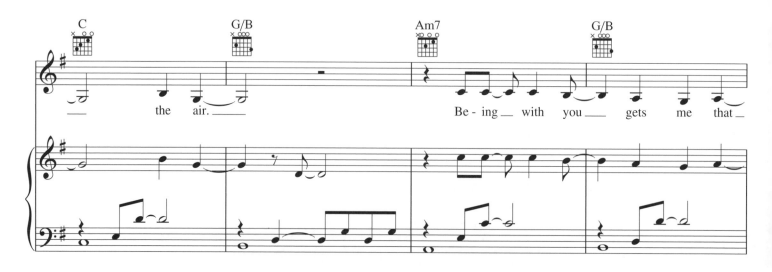

CAN'T YOU SEE

Words and Music by
TOY CALDWELL

Moderate Country Rock

I'm gon' take a freight train
Now, I'm gon-na find me
I'm gon-na buy me a tick-et now,

down at the sta-tion, Lord.___ I don't care___ where it goes.___
a hole in the wall.___ I'm gon' crawl in-side and die.___
as far as I can.___ I ain't nev-er com-ing back.___

Recorded a half step higher.

CHATTAHOOCHEE

Words and Music by JIM McBRIDE
and ALAN JACKSON

Way down yon - der on the Chat - ta - hoo - chee

Well, we fogged up the win - dows in ___ my old Chev - y;

COSMIC COWBOY

Words and Music by
MICHAEL MARTIN MURPHEY

To Coda ⊕

su - per - na - t'ral coun - try ___ rock - in' ga - loot. ___

Guitar solo

CITY OF NEW ORLEANS

Words and Music by
STEVE GOODMAN

Moderately bright Country, in 2

1. Rid-in' on ___ the Cit-y of ___ New Or - leans,
2., 3. (See additional lyrics)

Il-li-nois ___ Cen - tral Mon-day morn - in' rail. ___

Fif-teen cars ___ and fif - teen rest - less rid-

I'll be gone ___ five hun - dred miles ___ when the day ___ is done.

Additional Lyrics

2. Dealin' card games with the old men in the club car,
Penny a point ain't no one keepin' score.
Pass the paper bag that holds the bottle;
Feel the wheels grumblin' 'neath the floor;
And the sons of Pullman porters, and the sons of engineers
Ride their father's magic carpet made of steel.
Mothers with their babes asleep are rockin' to the gentle beat
And the rhythm of the rails is all they feel.

3. Night time on the City of New Orleans,
Changin' cars in Memphis, Tennessee;
Halfway home, we'll be there by mornin',
Thru the Mississippi darkness rollin' down to the sea.
But all the towns and people seem to fade into a bad dream,
And the steel rail still ain't heard the news;
The conductor sings his songs again;
The passengers will please refrain,
This train's got the disappearin' railroad blues.

THE DEVIL WENT DOWN TO GEORGIA

Words and Music by CHARLIE DANIELS,
JOHN THOMAS CRAIN, JR., WILLIAM JOEL DiGREGORIO,
FRED LAROY EDWARDS, CHARLES FRED HAYWARD
and JAMES WAINWRIGHT MARSHALL

The dev-il went down to Geor-gia. He was look-in' for a soul to steal. __ He was in a bind 'cause he was

The dev-il bowed his head be-cause he knew that he'd _ been beat. And he

laid that gold - en fid - dle on the ground _ at John - ny's feet.

John-ny said, "Dev - il, just come on back _ if you ev - er want to try a - gain. _ 'Cause I

D.S. al Coda

told you once, you son - of - a - gun, _ I'm the best that's ev - er been." _ He played,

DOWN AT THE TWIST AND SHOUT

Words and Music by
MARY CHAPIN CARPENTER

Fast Country Two-Beat

Sat-ur-day night __ and the moon is out. __ I wan-na head on o-ver to the Twist and Shout, find a two-step part-ner and a Ca-jun beat. When it lifts me up, __ I'm gon-na

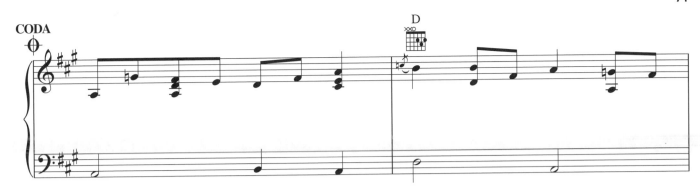

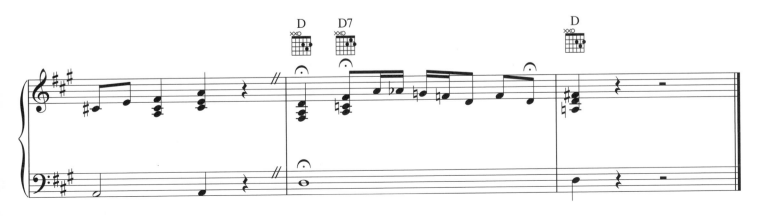

FEEL LIKE A ROCK STAR

Words and Music by RODNEY CLAWSON
and CHRISTOPHER TOMPKINS

Heavy Country Rock

Do you

smoke, do you drink, do you yell out, "Hank"? __ Do you fold it in your pock-et, do you lock it in the bank? Do you
kick the dirt or work a Ve-gas stop? ___ Do you hit __ the __ strip or roll a coun-try __ mile? Do you

Recorded a half step higher.

juice in the goose or the Coke in the Crown?   What - ev - er makes you feel like a

rock   star. _
(Vocal ad lib. on repeat)

Repeat and Fade

Optional Ending

EAST BOUND AND DOWN

from the Universal Film SMOKEY AND THE BANDIT

Words and Music by JERRY REED
and DICK FELLER

East bound and down, ___ load-ed up ___ and truck-in'. We're gon-na do what they ___ say can't ___ be done. ___

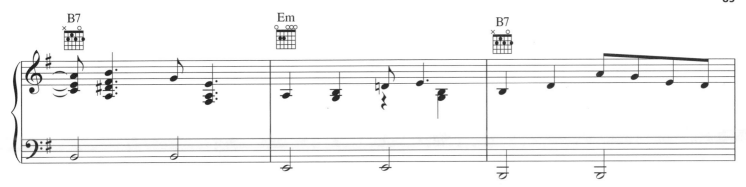

watch ol' Ban - dit run. _____

FOOLED AROUND AND FELL IN LOVE

Words and Music by
ELVIN BISHOP

FREE BIRD

Words and Music by ALLEN COLLINS
and RONNIE VAN ZANT

Slowly

If I leave__ here to-mor-row, would you still re-mem-ber
Bye, bye, ba-by, it's been a sweet love, though this feel-ing I can't

me? For I must be__ trav-'ling on now,
change. But please don't take__ it so bad-ly,

GUITARS, CADILLACS

Words and Music by
DWIGHT YOAKAM

There ain't no glam -

A GOOD HEARTED WOMAN

Words and Music by WILLIE NELSON
and WAYLON JENNINGS

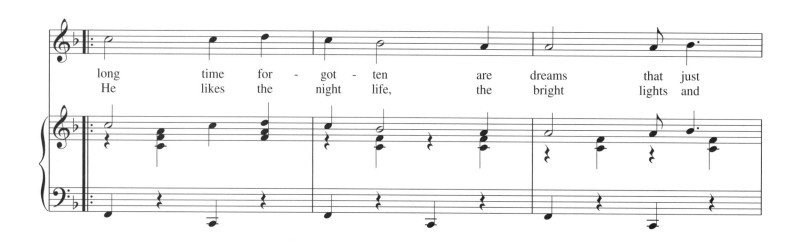

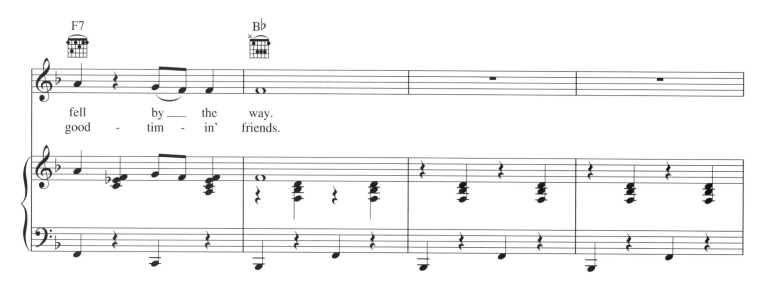

And the good life he prom-ised
When the par-ty's all o - ver

ain't what she's liv-ing _____ to - day. ___
she'll wel - come him back home a - gain. ___

Lord knows she
But she

nev - er com - plains of the bad times or ___
don't un - der - stand him, but she does the ___

good - heart - ed wom - an ___ in love with a good - tim - in'

man.

She

loves him in spite of his ways that she don't un - der -

stand.

Through

HERE'S A QUARTER
(Call Someone Who Cares)

Words and Music by
TRAVIS TRITT

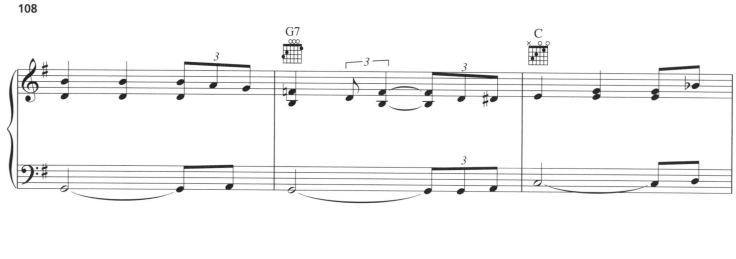

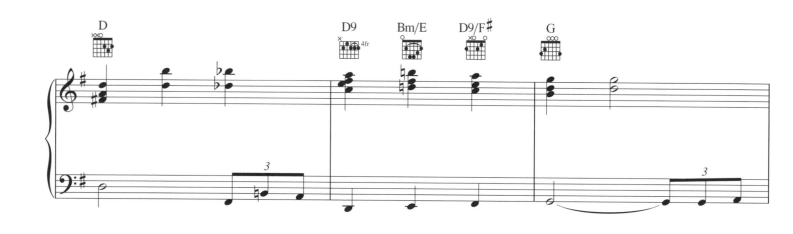

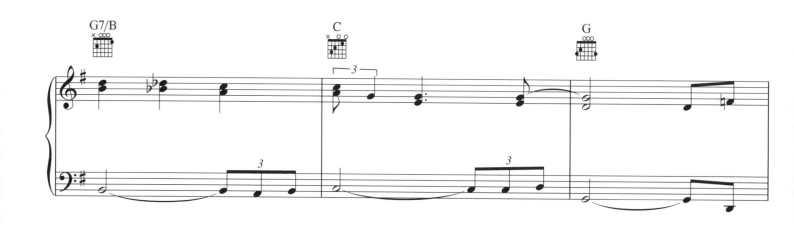

HEARD IT IN A LOVE SONG

Words and Music by
TOY CALDWELL

Moderately

I ain't nev-er been with a wom-an long e-nough
I'm the kind of man
I'm gon-na be leav-in'
I nev-er had a damn thing, but what I had

for my boots to get old. _____
who likes to get his way. _____
at the break of dawn. _____
I had to leave it be - hind. _____

We been _____ to - geth - er so long _____ now, they
Like _____ to start _____ dream - in' 'bout _____ to -
Wish you _____ could come, _____ but I don't need no
You're the hard - est thing _____ I ev - er _____ tried to

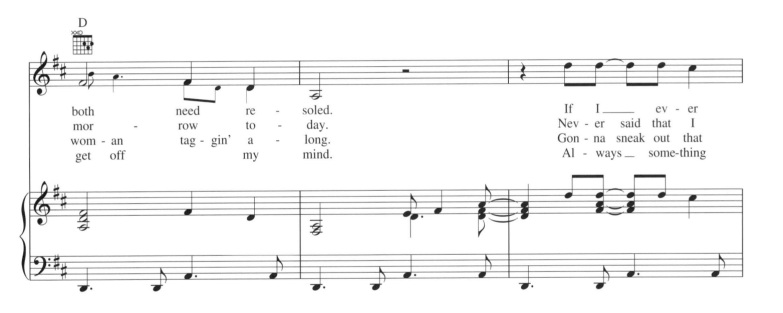

both _____ need re - soled.
mor - row to - day.
wom - an tag - gin' a - long.
get off my mind.

If I _____ ev - er
Nev - er said that I
Gon - na sneak out that
Al - ways _____ some-thing

set - tle down, _____ you'd be my kind. _____
love you, e - ven though it's so. _____
door; _____ could - n't stand to see you cry. _____
green - er on _____ the oth - er side of that hill. _____

And it's a
There's that
I'd stay an -
I was born a

112

HEARTACHE TONIGHT

Words and Music by JOHN DAVID SOUTHER,
DON HENLEY, GLENN FREY
and BOB SEGER

heart - ache to - night, I know.

HELP ME MAKE IT THROUGH THE NIGHT

Words and Music by
KRIS KRISTOFFERSON

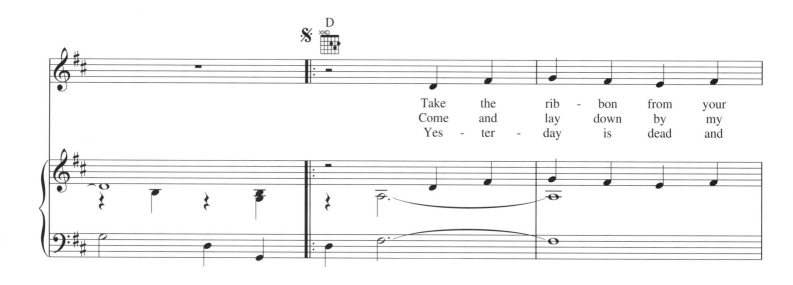

Take the rib-bon from your
Come and lay down by my
Yes-ter-day is dead and

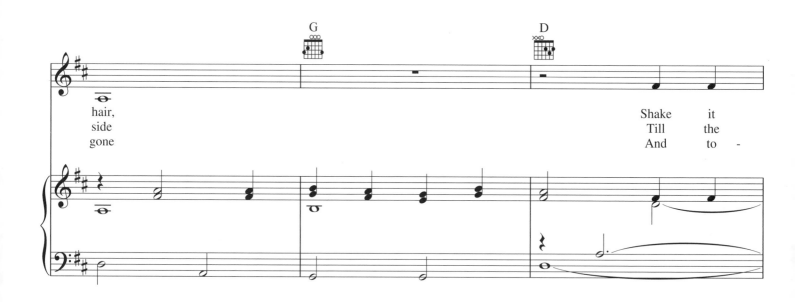

hair,
side
gone

Shake it
Till the
And to-

HOTEL CALIFORNIA

Words and Music by DON HENLEY,
GLENN FREY and DON FELDER

JACKSON

Words and Music by BILLY EDD WHEELER
and JERRY LEIBER

(1.,5.) We got mar - ried in a fe - ver,
(2.) go on, my _____ sweet dad - dy,
(3.) I breeze in - to that cit - y,
(4.) laugh at you _____ in Jack - son,   I'll be

hot - ter than a pep - per sprout. _____
go a - head and wreck your health. _____
peo - ple gon - na scrape and bow. _____
danc - in' on a po - ny keg. _____   Then I'll

We been talk - in' 'bout Jack - son
Play your hand ___ like a lov - er man, ___ make a
All them wom - en gon - na beg me,
lead you 'round town ___ like a scold - ed hound ___ with your

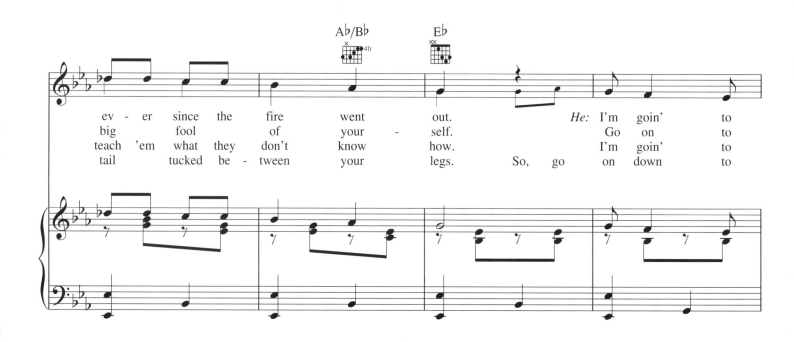

Ab/Bb   **Eb**

ev - er since the fire went out. *He:* I'm goin' to
big fool of your - self. Go on to
teach 'em what they don't know how. I'm goin' to
tail tucked be - tween your legs. So, go on down to

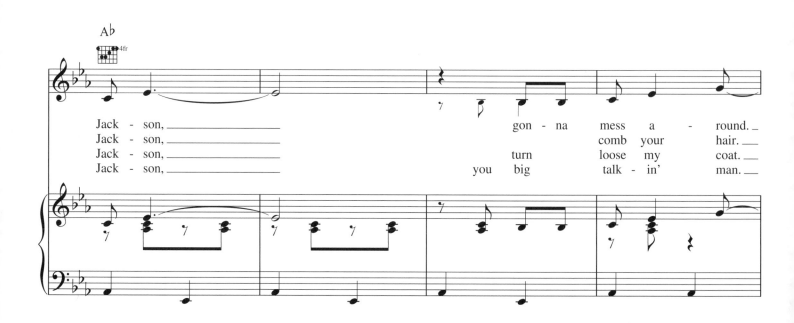

Ab

Jack - son, ___ gon - na mess a - round.
Jack - son, ___ comb your hair. ___
Jack - son, ___ turn loose my coat. ___
Jack - son, ___ you big talk - in' man. ___

IF YOU WANNA GET TO HEAVEN

Words and Music by STEVE CASH
and JOHN DILLON

IF YOU'RE GOING THROUGH HELL
(Before the Devil Even Knows)

Words and Music by ANNIE TATE,
SAM TATE and DAVE BERG

If you're

dev - il   e - ven   knows   you're   there. _____

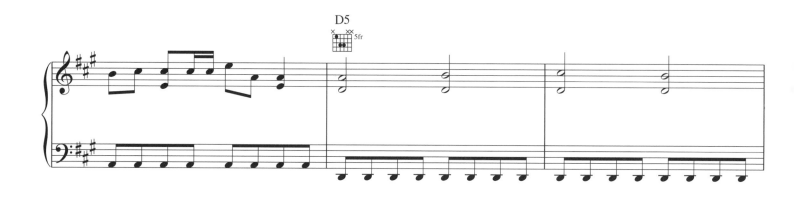

LIFE IN THE FAST LANE

Words and Music by DON HENLEY,
GLENN FREY and JOE WALSH

Moderate Rock beat

He was a hard-head-ed man.___ He was bru-tal-ly hand-some,
Keyed up for ac-tion and hot for the game, the

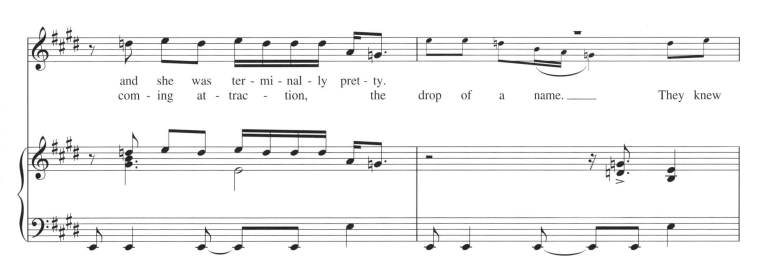

and she was ter-mi-nal-ly pret-ty.
com-ing at-trac-tion, the drop of a name.___ They knew

She held him up, and he held her for ran - som in the heart
all the right peo - ple, they took all the right pills._____ They threw

_____ of the cold, cold___ cit - y.
out - ra - geous par - ties, they paid heav - en - ly bills. He had a
There were

A7

nas - ty rep - u - ta - tion as a cru - el dude.___ They
lines on the mir - ror, lines on her face. She pre -

said he was ruth - less, they said he was crude. _____ They had
tend - ed not to no - tice, she was caught up in the ___ race.

one thing in com - mon: they were good in bed. _____ She'd say,
Out in the eve - ning un - til it was light, he was

"Fast - er, fast - er. The lights are turn - in' red." _____
too tired to make ___ it; she was too tired to fight a - bout it.

To Coda

Life in the fast lane, uh - huh.

Load - ed and burn - in', blind - ed by thirst, they

did - n't see the stop sign; took a turn for the worse. She said,

"Lis - ten, ba - by, you can hear the en - gine ring. We've been

A LITTLE LESS TALK
AND A LOT MORE ACTION

Words and Music by KEITH HINTON
and JIMMY ALAN STEWART

lit - tle less talk __ and a lot more ac - tion. *Guitar solo*

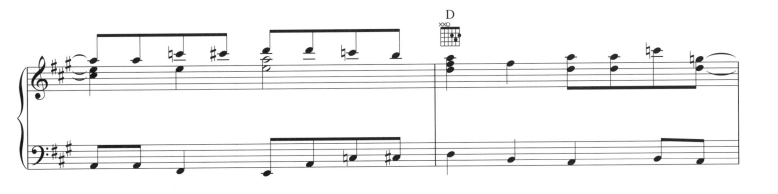

LITTLE SISTER

Words and Music by DOC POMUS
and MORT SHUMAN

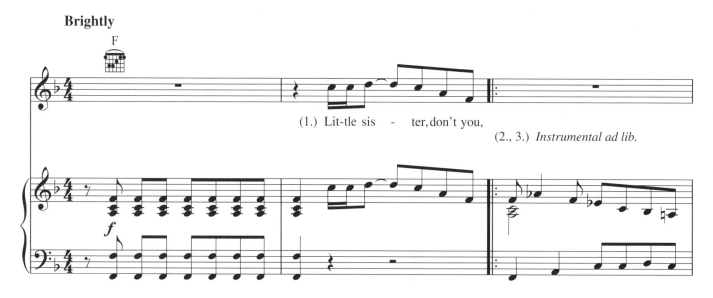

(1.) Lit-tle sis - ter, don't you,

(2., 3.) *Instrumental ad lib.*

lit - tle sis - ter, don't you,

lit - tle sis - ter, don't you

kiss me once or twice, tell____ me that it's nice and then you run.____

LYIN' EYES

Words and Music by DON HENLEY
and GLENN FREY

Lyrics:

City girls just seem to find out early __ how to o - pen __ doors __ with just a smile. __

She get up __ just and seem pours her - self __ a strong __ one, __ and stares out __ at the stars __ up in the sky. __

MOUNTAIN MUSIC

Words and Music by
RANDY OWEN

ME AND BOBBY McGEE

Words and Music by KRIS KRISTOFFERSON
and FRED FOSTER

Busted flat in Baton Rouge, waitin' for a train, when I's feel-in' near as fad-ed as my jeans. Bob-by thumbed a die-sel down just be-fore it rained. It rode us all the way in-to New Or-leans. I

Vocal written one octave higher than sung.

Lord.

La la la____ la la____ la la____ la la____ la la____

____ la la____ la la,____ hey, hey, hey, Bob-by Mc - Gee,____ ah.

NEW KID IN TOWN

Words and Music by JOHN DAVID SOUTHER,
DON HENLEY and GLENN FREY

Moderately

There's talk on the street; __
You look in her eyes; __

__ it sounds so fa - mil - liar.
__ the mu - sic be - gins to play.

Great ex- pec- ta- tions, ev-'ry-bod-y's watch-ing you.

Hope-less ro- man- tics, here we go a- gain.

Peo- ple you meet, they all seem to know

But af -ter a while you're look- ing the oth -

____ you. It's those

____ er way.

E - ven your old ____

rest - less ____

____ friends treat you like you're some-thing new.

____ hearts that nev- er mend.

NINE TO FIVE

Words and Music by
DOLLY PARTON

ON THE ROAD AGAIN

Words and Music by
WILLIE NELSON

ONE STEP OVER THE LINE

Words and Music by
JOHN HIATT

PEACEFUL EASY FEELING

Words and Music by
JACK TEMPCHIN

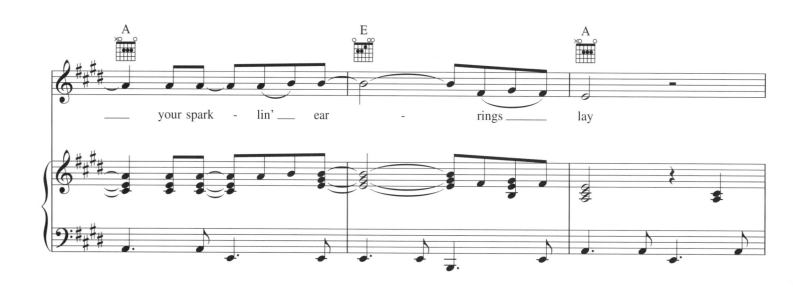

Whoa.

rit.

RAMBLIN' MAN

Words and Music by
DICKEY BETTS

Brightly

Lord, I ___ was born ___ a ram - blin' man, _____ try'n' to make a liv - in' and do - in' the best I ____ can. ___ And

QUEEN OF HEARTS

Words and Music by
HANK DEVITO

Mid - night,_____ and I'm wait - ing on the twelve - o -
Ba - by,_____ you know it____ makes me
Lov - ers,_____ I know you've____ had____ a

that's what I have to do _____ to keep me a - way from you. _____

ROCK MY WORLD
(Little Country Girl)

Words and Music by BILL LABOUNTY
and STEVE O'BRIEN

She's got a T-top Ca-ma-ro with a scoop on the hood ___ and

Rock __ my __ world. __

D.S. al Coda

Rock my ___ world, ___

lit - tle

Repeat and Fade

coun - try girl. ___

Optional Ending

coun - try girl. ___

RUBY, DON'T TAKE YOUR LOVE TO TOWN

Words and Music by
MEL TILLIS

THE SOUTH'S GONNA DO IT

Words and Music by
CHARLIE DANIELS

to a reb-el 'cause the South's gon-na do it a-gain ___ and a-gain.

Instrumental solo - ad lib.

Instrumental solo - ad lib.

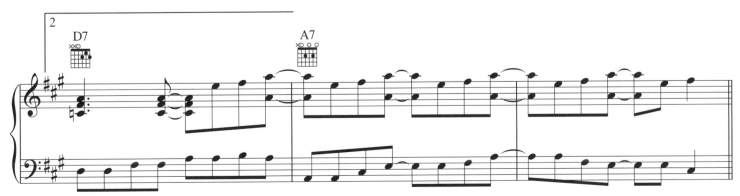

SWEET HOME ALABAMA

Words and Music by RONNIE VAN ZANT,
ED KING and GARY ROSSINGTON

TAKE IT EASY

Words and Music by JACKSON BROWNE
and GLENN FREY

TAKE THIS JOB AND SHOVE IT

Words and Music by
DAVID ALLEN COE

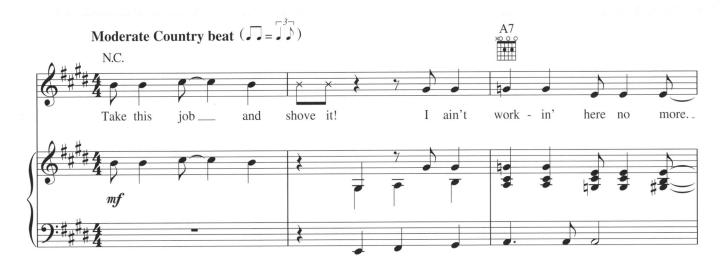

TENNESSEE RIVER

Words and Music by
RANDY OWEN

Moderately, in 2

I was born _____ a - cross ___ the riv - er

in the moun - tains _____ where I ____ call ___ home.

Lord, times were good ___ there. _____ Don't ___ know why

love _____ can still be found. Oh, Ten-nes-see

D.S. al Coda

CODA

Oh, Ten-nes-see Riv - er. _____

Fast

Oh, Ten-nes-see

TRAIN, TRAIN

Words and Music by
SHORTY MEDLOCKE

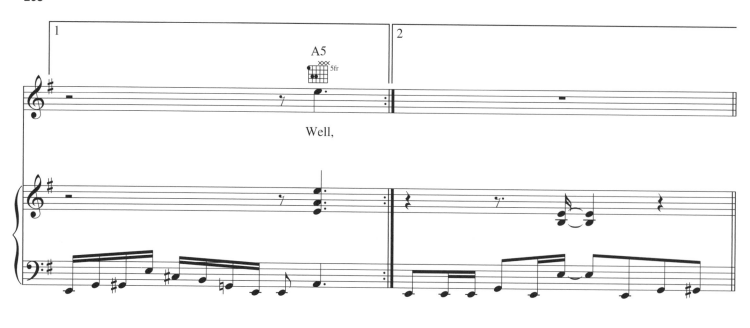

Well,

Instrumental solo - ad lib.

Solo ends   Well,   good - bye, _____   pret - ty

UP ON CRIPPLE CREEK

Words and Music by
ROBBIE ROBERTSON

1. When I get off ___ of this moun-tain, ya
2.-5. *(See additional lyrics)*

know where I wan-na go?

Straight down ___ the Mis-

-sis-sip-pi Riv-er to the Gulf of Mex-i-co to

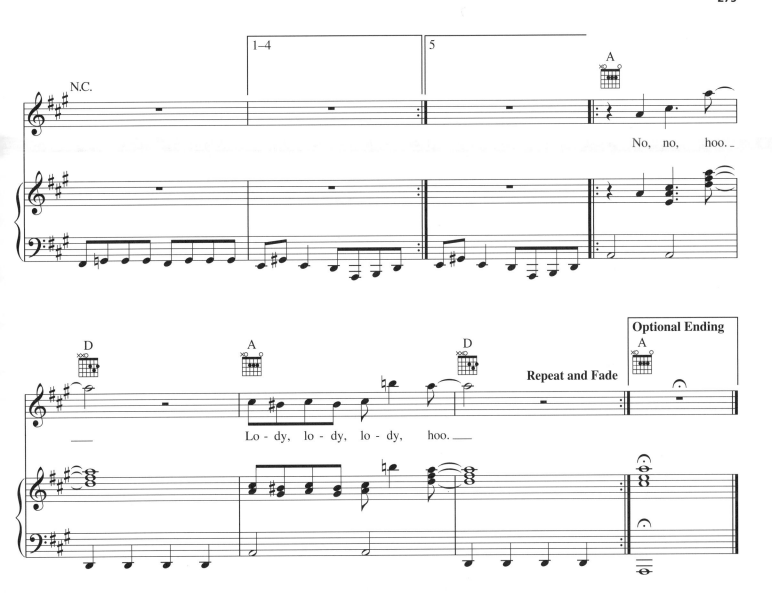

Additional Lyrics

2. Good luck had just stung me; to the racetrack I did go.
   She bet on one horse to win and I bet on another to show.
   The odds were in my favor; I had 'em five to one.
   When that nag to win came around the track, sure enough we had won.
   Chorus

3. I took up all of my winnings and I gave my little Bessie half.
   She tore it up and threw it in my face just for a laugh.
   Now, there's one thing in the whole wide world I sure would like to see:
   That's when the little love of mine dips her doughnut in my tea.
   Chorus

4. Now, me and my mate were back at the shack; we had Spike Jones on the box.
   She said, "I can't take the way he sings, but I love to hear him talk,"
   Now, that just gave my heart a throb to the bottom of my feet,
   And I swore as I took another pull, my Bessie can't be beat.
   Chorus

5. There's a flood out in California, and up north it's freezing cold,
   And this living off the road is getting pretty old.
   So I guess I'll call up my big mama, tell her I'll be rolling in.
   But you know, deep down, I'm kind of tempted to go and see my Bessie again.
   Chorus

T-R-O-U-B-L-E

Words and Music by
JERRY CHESNUT

2. I was a lit - tle bit - ty ba - by when my
3.,4. *(See additional lyrics)*

pa - pa hit the skids. Ma - ma had a time tryin' to raise nine kids.

Told me not to stare 'cause it was im - po - lite, ___ and did the best she could to try to

Additional Lyrics

3. Well, you talk about a woman, I've seen a lotta others,
   With too much somethin' and not enough of another.
   Lookin' like glory and walkin' like a dream.
   CHORUS: Mother Nature's sure been good to Y-O-U.
   Well, your mother musta been another good lookin' mother, too.
   Say, hey, good L-double O-K-I-N-G, I smell T-R-O-U-B-L-E.

4. Well, you talk about a troublemakin' hunka pokey bait
   The men are gonna love, and all the women gonna hate,
   Remindin' them of everything they're never gonna be.
   Maybe the beginnin' of a World War Three.
   CHORUS: 'Cause the world ain't ready for nothing like a Y-O-U.
   I bet your mother musta been another somethin' or the other, too.
   Say, hey, good L-double O-K-I-N-G, I smell T-R-O-U-B-L-E.

TUFF ENUFF

Words and Music by
KIM WILSON

1. I would walk ten___ miles on my___
2. For you___ ba-by, I would___
3.,4. *(See additional lyrics)*

hands and knees.___ Ain't no doubt a-bout___ it ba-by, it's you I aim to please.___ I'd
swim the sea.___ Noth-in' I'd do for___ you that's___ too tuff for me.___ I'd put

tuff e - nuff? _ Ain't _ that tuff e - nuff, _

Repeat and Fade

ain't _ that tuff e - nuff? _ Ain't _ that

Additional lyrics

3. I'd work twenty-four hours, seven days a week
   Just so I could come come and kiss your cheek.
   I love you in the morning and I love you at noon,
   I love you in the night and take you to the moon.
   Chorus

4. I'd lay in a pile of burning money that I've earned
   And not even worry about getting burned.
   I'd climb the Empire State Building, fight Muhammad Ali
   Just to have you, baby, close to me.
   Chorus

WHISKEY RIVER

Words and Music by
J.B. SHINN III

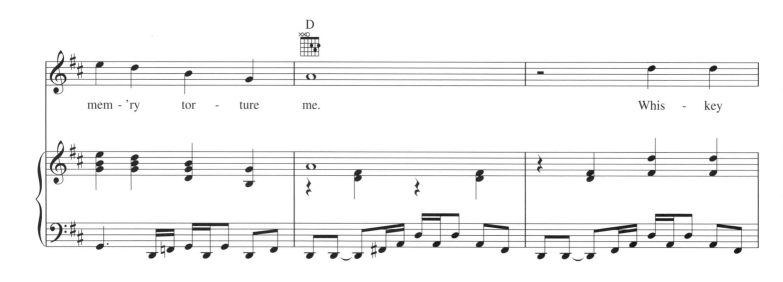

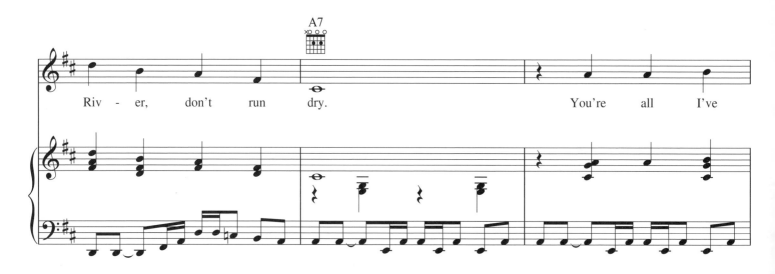

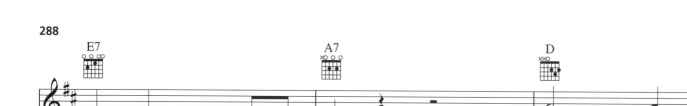

wet - ness of its soul. Feel - ing the

am - ber cur - rent flow - in' from my mind,

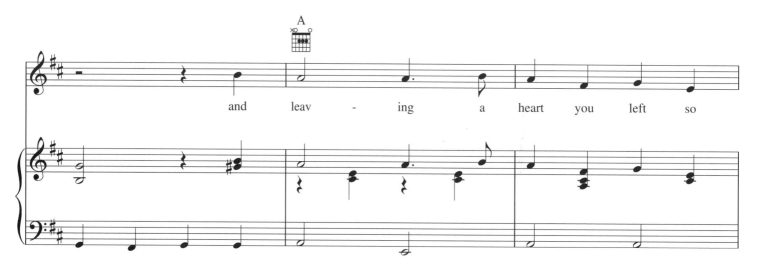

and leav - ing a heart you left so

cold. Whis - key

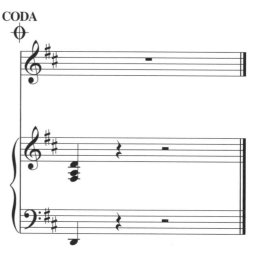

YOUR MAMA DON'T DANCE

Words and Music by JIM MESSINA
and KENNY LOGGINS

YOU'RE STILL THE ONE

Words and Music by SHANIA TWAIN
and R.J. LANGE

THE BEST EVER

COLLECTION
ARRANGED FOR PIANO, VOICE AND GUITAR

150 of the Most Beautiful Songs Ever
150 ballads
00360735 ....$27.00

150 More of the Most Beautiful Songs Ever
150 songs
00311318 ....$29.99

More of the Best Acoustic Rock Songs Ever
69 tunes
00311738 ....$19.95

Best Acoustic Rock Songs Ever
65 acoustic hits
00310984 ....$19.95

Best Big Band Songs Ever
68 big band hits
00359129 ....$17.99

Best Blues Songs Ever
73 blues tunes
00312874 ....$19.99

Best Broadway Songs Ever
83 songs
00309155 ....$24.99

More of the Best Broadway Songs Ever
82 songs
00311501 ....$22.95

Best Children's Songs Ever
102 tunes
00310360 (Easy Piano) $19.95

Best Christmas Songs Ever
69 holiday favorites
00359130 ....$24.99

Best Classic Rock Songs Ever
64 hits
00310800 ....$19.99

Best Classical Music Ever
86 classical favorites
00310674 (Piano Solo) $19.95

Best Country Songs Ever
78 classic country hits
00359135 ....$19.99

Best Disco Songs Ever
50 songs
00312565 ....$19.99

Best Dixieland Songs Ever
90 songs
00312326 ....$19.99

Best Early Rock 'n' Roll Songs Ever
74 songs
00310816 ....$19.95

Best Easy Listening Songs Ever
75 mellow favorites
00359193 ....$19.95

Best Gospel Songs Ever
80 gospel songs
00310503 ....$19.99

Best Hymns Ever
118 hymns
00310774 ....$18.99

Best Jazz Standards Ever
77 jazz hits
00311641 ....$19.95

More of the Best Jazz Standards Ever
74 beloved jazz hits
00311023 ....$19.95

Best Latin Songs Ever
67 songs
00310355 ....$19.99

Best Love Songs Ever
65 favorite love songs
00359198 ....$19.95

Best Movie Songs Ever
71 songs
00310063 ....$19.95

Best Praise & Worship Songs Ever
80 all-time favorites
00311057 ....$22.99

More of the Best Praise & Worship Songs Ever
76 songs
00311800 ....$24.99

Best R&B Songs Ever
66 songs
00310184 ....$19.95

Best Rock Songs Ever
63 songs
00490424 ....$18.95

Best Songs Ever
72 must-own classics
00359224 ....$24.99

Best Soul Songs Ever
70 hits
00311427 ....$19.95

Best Standards Ever, Vol. 1 (A-L)
72 beautiful ballads
00359231 ....$17.95

Best Standards Ever, Vol. 2 (M-Z)
73 songs
00359232 ....$17.99

More of the Best Standards Ever, Vol. 1 (A-L)
76 all-time favorites
00310813 ....$17.95

More of the Best Standards Ever, Vol. 2 (M-Z)
75 stunning standards
00310814 ....$17.95

Best Torch Songs Ever
70 sad and sultry favorites
00311027 ....$19.95

Best Wedding Songs Ever
70 songs
00311096 ....$19.95

Prices, contents and availability subject to change without notice. Not all products available outside the U.S.A.

7777 W. BLUEMOUND RD. P.O. BOX 13819 MILWAUKEE, WI 53213

Visit us online for complete songlists at
www.halleonard.com

THE GRAMMY AWARDS
SONGBOOKS FROM HAL LEONARD

These elite collections of the nominees and winners of Grammy Awards since the honor's inception in 1958 provide a snapshot of the changing times in popular music.

PIANO/VOCAL/GUITAR

GRAMMY AWARDS RECORD OF THE YEAR 1958–2011
Beat It • Beautiful Day • Bridge over Troubled Water • Don't Know Why • Don't Worry, Be Happy • The Girl from Ipanema (Garôta De Ipanema) • Hotel California • I Will Always Love You • Just the Way You Are • Mack the Knife • Moon River • My Heart Will Go on (Love Theme from 'Titanic') • Rehab • Sailing • Unforgettable • Up, Up and Away • The Wind Beneath My Wings • and more.
00313603 P/V/G.......................................$19.99

THE GRAMMY AWARDS SONG OF THE YEAR 1958–1969
Battle of New Orleans • Born Free • Fever • The Good Life • A Hard Day's Night • Harper Valley P.T.A. • Hello, Dolly! • Hey Jude • King of the Road • Little Green Apples • Mrs. Robinson • Ode to Billy Joe • People • Somewhere, My Love • Strangers in the Night • A Time for Us (Love Theme) • Volare • Witchcraft • Yesterday • and more.
00313598 P/V/G.......................................$19.99

THE GRAMMY AWARDS SONG OF THE YEAR 1970–1979
Alone Again (Naturally) • American Pie • At Seventeen • Don't It Make My Brown Eyes Blue • Honesty • (I Never Promised You A) Rose Garden • I Write the Songs • Killing Me Softly with His Song • Let It Be • Me and Bobby McGee • Send in the Clowns • Song Sung Blue • Stayin' Alive • Three Times a Lady • The Way We Were • You're So Vain • You've Got a Friend • and more.
00313599 P/V/G.......................................$19.99

THE GRAMMY AWARDS SONG OF THE YEAR 1980–1989
Against All Odds (Take a Look at Me Now) • Always on My Mind • Beat It • Bette Davis Eyes • Don't Worry, Be Happy • Ebony and Ivory • Endless Love • Every Breath You Take • Eye of the Tiger • Fame • Fast Car • Hello • I Just Called to Say I Love You • La Bamba • Nine to Five • The Rose • Somewhere Out There • Time After Time • We Are the World • and more.
00313600 P/V/G.......................................$19.99

THE GRAMMY AWARDS SONG OF THE YEAR 1990–1999
Can You Feel the Love Tonight • (Everything I Do) I Do It for You • From a Distance • Give Me One Reason • I Swear • Kiss from a Rose • Losing My Religion • My Heart Will Go on (Love Theme from 'Titanic') • Nothing Compares 2 U • Smooth • Streets of Philadelphia • Tears in Heaven • Unforgettable • Walking in Memphis • A Whole New World • You Oughta Know • and more.
00313601 P/V/G.......................................$19.99

THE GRAMMY AWARDS SONG OF THE YEAR 2000–2009
Beautiful • Beautiful Day • Breathe • Chasing Pavements • Complicated • Dance with My Father • Daughters • Don't Know Why • Fallin' • I Hope You Dance • I'm Yours • Live like You Were Dying • Poker Face • Rehab • Single Ladies (Put a Ring on It) • A Thousand Miles • Umbrella • Use Somebody • Viva La Vida • and more.
00313602 P/V/G.......................................$19.99

THE GRAMMY AWARDS BEST COUNTRY SONG 1964–2011
Always on My Mind • Before He Cheats • Behind Closed Doors • Bless the Broken Road • Butterfly Kisses • Dang Me • Forever and Ever, Amen • The Gambler • I Still Believe in You • I Swear • King of the Road • Live like You Were Dying • Love Can Build a Bridge • Need You Now • On the Road Again • White Horse • You Decorated My Life • and more.
00313604 P/V/G.......................................$19.99

THE GRAMMY AWARDS BEST R&B SONG 1958–2011
After the Love Has Gone • Ain't No Sunshine • Be Without You • Billie Jean • End of the Road • Good Golly Miss Molly • Hit the Road Jack • If You Don't Know Me by Now • Papa's Got a Brand New Bag • Respect • Shine • Single Ladies (Put a Ring on It) • (Sittin' On) the Dock of the Bay • Superstition • U Can't Touch This • We Belong Together • and more.
00313605 P/V/G.......................................$19.99

THE GRAMMY AWARDS BEST POP & ROCK GOSPEL ALBUMS (2000–2011)
Call My Name • Come on Back to Me • Deeper Walk • Forever • Gone • I Need You • I Smile • I Will Follow • King • Leaving 99 • Lifesong • Looking Back at You • Much of You • My Love Remains • Say So • Somebody's Watching • Step by Step/Forever We Will Sing • Tunnel • Unforgetful You • You Hold My World • Your Love Is a Song • and more.
00313680 P/V/G.......................................$16.99

ELECTRONIC KEYBOARD

THE GRAMMY AWARDS RECORD OF THE YEAR 1958–2011 – VOL. 160
All I Wanna Do • Bridge over Troubled Water • Don't Know Why • The Girl from Ipanema (Garôta De Ipanema) • Hotel California • I Will Always Love You • Just the Way You Are • Killing Me Softly with His Song • Love Will Keep Us Together • Rehab • Unforgettable • What's Love Got to Do with It • The Wind Beneath My Wings • and more.
00100315 E-Z Play Today #160 ....$16.99

PRO VOCAL
WOMEN'S EDITIONS

THE GRAMMY AWARDS BEST FEMALE POP VOCAL PERFORMANCE 1990–1999 — VOL. 57
Book/CD Pack
All I Wanna Do • Building a Mystery • Constant Craving • I Will Always Love You • I Will Remember You • My Heart Will Go on (Love Theme from 'Titanic') • No More "I Love You's" • Something to Talk About (Let's Give Them Something to Talk About) • Unbreak My Heart • Vision of Love.
00740446 Melody/Lyrics/Chords................$14.99

THE GRAMMY AWARDS BEST FEMALE POP VOCAL PERFORMANCE 2000-2009 – VOL. 58
Book/CD Pack
Ain't No Other Man • Beautiful • Chasing Pavements • Don't Know Why • Halo • I Try • I'm like a Bird • Rehab • Since U Been Gone • Sunrise.
00740447 Melody/Lyrics/Chords................$14.99

MEN'S EDITIONS

THE GRAMMY AWARDS BEST MALE POP VOCAL PERFORMANCE 1990-1999 – VOL. 59
Book/CD Pack
Brand New Day • Can You Feel the Love Tonight • Candle in the Wind 1997 • Change the World • If I Ever Lose My Faith in You • Kiss from a Rose • My Father's Eyes • Oh, Pretty Woman • Tears in Heaven • When a Man Loves a Woman.
00740448 Melody/Lyrics/Chords................$14.99

THE GRAMMY AWARDS BEST MALE POP VOCAL PERFORMANCE 2000-2009 – VOL. 60
Book/CD Pack
Cry Me a River • Daughters • Don't Let Me Be Lonely Tonight • Make It Mine • Say • Waiting on the World to Change • What Goes Around...Comes Around Interlude • Your Body Is a Wonderland.
00740449 Melody/Lyrics/Chords................$14.99

Prices, contents, and availabilbity subject to change without notice.

HAL•LEONARD® CORPORATION
7777 W. BLUEMOUND RD. P.O. BOX 13819 MILWAUKEE, WI 53213

www.halleonard.com

0713